21 Things I Thought

Toni-Marie Turney

BookLeaf
Publishing

Presentation by *BookLeaf Publishing*

Web: www.bookleafpub.com

E-mail: info@bookleafpub.com

ISBN: 9789357697132

First edition 2023

DEDICATION

I dedicate this book to the people who commit themselves to massive projects, despite having little knowledge of how to do them. Because same.

ACKNOWLEDGEMENT

I want to thank myself for not giving up on this, even when it would have been easier. (I know that's not what this is for, but the people around me made writing more difficult because they kept interrupting. I still love them all.)

One

One day
I wish to be
Nothing more
And nothing less
Than Me.

Two

Two would be wrong
If you are trying to say also
Even if you mean you had one
And then another one too
Then that would make two
But two doesn't mean also
And too isn't a number
And neither two nor too
Mean the same as to.

Three

Apparently
Three times is the charm
Which sounds lucky
But it's not always
It generally means
If you failed twice
You'll probably succeed
On the third try
Which could mean anything
From
Successfully turning the key in a stiff lock
The third time you try
To
Smashing your phone screen
The third time you drop it
It could be a curse
Or a blessing
So is the
Third time lucky?

Four

There's something about four
That feels incredibly satisfying
Not only because it's even
But because it's so useful
It's smooth
It's clean
It's functional
If you look around a room
There are many fours
Hidden within
Things with four sides
And four corners
A box
A wall
A door
Most of them made of fours
Because it works.

Five

Five days
Is a working week
Five nights
Is a nice holiday
I need more nights.

Six

I miss being six
Life was easier then
I could spend all day colouring
Or build a den
And no one would tell me
It was a waste of time
Because what else would I do
When I was only six.

Seven

7 is my favourite number
But seven looks odd
Maybe it's because
When I write my birth date
It's 7th February 1997
Or 07/02/1997
It's never seven
February is my favourite month too
Partly because it brings my favourite 7th
But also because
It brought my husband to be
And we became a couple
On 18/02/14
If you take the 1 from the 8
That makes 7
If you add the 2, 1 and 4
That also makes 7
It may sound ridiculous
But I think that's a good reason
For seven to be my favourite number
And winter my favourite season.

Eight

I was only eight
When I started to worry
About my weight
There was a boy
In the year above
Who copied me
When I had my mouth full
I took too big a bite
And was trying to chew
He called my name
And puffed out his cheeks
He thought it was funny
And his friends laughed too.

Nine

It takes nine months
For a baby to grow
From particles
Too small to see
Into a human being
It's fascinating
Really
How someone who
Didn't exist
Can take only
Nine months
To be.

Ten

A decade
Is a long time
Most people live
Between six and eight
Some live nine
Some live five
Or less
Very few
Live Ten.

Eleven

I find it funny
That eleven has even
In its name when
It is
In fact
Odd.

Twelve

I was twelve
When my grandma died
I wish I'd been older
That I'd had more time
I wish she'd lived longer
That she'd had more time
I used to write her letters
To tell her about my life
She'd write back
To tell me about hers
Sometimes I think
I should write to her again
But I know she won't reply
And she didn't leave an address
For my letter to be sent
Sometimes I wonder
Where it is
That she went.

Thirteen

Life is filled with
Contradictions
And many are faced
At only thirteen
Bodies are changing
Minds are maturing
Some get leaner
Some get meaner
And all are told
That they are no longer
A child
But they're also not yet
Grown-up
They feel like they should
Get to be themselves
To have an opinion
And stand out from the crowd
But they daren't too much
Or they won't fit in
And they don't want to end up
At the bottom of the social bin
Every thirteen year old
Will struggle
And despite their complaints
They still need a cuddle.

Fourteen

Fourteen days
Is a fortnight
But if you ask
What a fortnight is
Most will say
Two weeks
And some will say
A game.

Fifteen

I thought I was smart
When I was fifteen
Sophisticated
Mature
Wise beyond my years
Now
At twenty-five
I know I was wrong.

Sixteen

I have never
Understood
Why sixteen is
Sweet
Or why it's only
Girls
Who are labelled as such
Honestly
It just feels
Creepy
Like there's something
Hiding
In the words that
No-one
Is willing to
Say
But they want it to be
Known.

Seventeen

The problem with
Being seventeen
Is that you aren't
An adult
So you don't have
Freedom
Or control over your
Own life
But you are expected
To make decisions
And look after
Yourself
As though you do
So you have someone
Telling you
That it is up to you
But the same person
Will criticise
When you don't make
The same decision that
They would do.

Eighteen

The first eighteen years
Of my life
Felt so long
At the time
Now I
Look back
And they weren't
Long enough.

Nineteen

Most people have had
Their first job
By nineteen
Some will have
Stayed there
Some will have
Moved on
But almost all
Will agree
That working until
You're seventy
Is working far
Too long.

Twenty

Some old people will tell you
Whether you ask them or not
By the time they
Were twenty
They were married
With a house and children
They'll say it like
You could do the same
Easily
If you only put down
Your phone
And stopped watching tv
The reality is
That's just not true
But if you try to explain it
They won't listen
To you.

Twenty-One

I went to London to celebrate
When I turned twenty-one
Anxiety ruined some of the trip
Making my bum sweaty
And my head heavy
No matter how hard
I tried
I couldn't pull myself
Out
The lights were
Too bright
And I was filled with
Self-doubt
I enjoyed the rest
The best that I could
I can't remember a lot of it
And I know that I should
I felt guilty about it
Until I found out
That the cause of my
Anxiety
Wasn't me
It was undiagnosed
ADHD.